150 WAYS TO MAKE MONEY ONLINE

BY TIMO HOFSTEE

Contents

Copyright

Introduction

I have been using the internet right from the beginning or to be more precise, using the World Wide Web. Now this book isn't about the history of the internet. But to resume it in a couple of words: in the 50's a network was created, based on the TCP/IP protocol. On top of that network were running a number of applications, like email. It was only in the early 90's that the first websites appeared, with all that goes with it, like browsers, search engines etc. And in today's world, when people talk about "the internet", they actually mean the usage of all these web sites.

And I have used the internet in my day to day job for decades. Just as the average user similar to millions of people are using it in their day-to-day life. Which is for the most part: sending and receiving emails, Facebook, Twitter, buying something online and maybe some random reading of some blogs , newspapers or some other subject that interests them.

And you cannot think about ANY subject or you will be able to find at least some information about it. In the years 2004-2006 I ran my own shop on Ebay. But at that time, I didn't dive really into the commercial side of the internet. I was just putting up listings and shipping out the products. I don't remember having done anything about what is called SEO (Search Engine Optimization). And I completely ignored all the ways people were using the internet to make money.

Until the day came, that I found myself out of a job, and started to investigate all the different ways to make money online. And this book is the result of that research. Of course, it would go way too far to develop every item in detail. The whole idea behind this book is to show that there are lots of ways to earn some money by using the internet.

Now let's make things clear. I haven't tried all these things myself. Actually some of them I was really surprised myself that they even existed.

What this book is NOT about

-This book, will not give you a 'ready-to-execute' business plan for all the ideas mentioned.

-This book will not teach you THE best and THE only way to make money online. And even less, how to do this fast.

-This book will not cover pyramid schemes

-This book will not cover MLM (Multi Level Marketing) practices.

Getting into an online business is…. Well, a business. And in that sense, it is very similar to an offline business or a brick and mortar shop. Yes, in the real world you can also make a quick buck by finding a job at McDonalds or distributing newspapers. And if your objective is to only find a way to make the $100 or $200 a month, because that's what you're short off every end of the month, that's fine.

However, if you're objective is to create a fulltime income, then you very likely have to put in fulltime work. There are no shortcuts to fast success online as there aren't any in the offline world. If they existed, this 'system' would be known by everybody but this would defeat its purpose.

Imagine that someone had a 'system' that would make you win at the lottery. Guaranteed. What would happen? IF it would work, in no time everybody would be playing this system. And what would happen? There is a pot of 10 million dollars and all 10 million players have the winning combination. Result: the 'system' has killed itself.

So, if you are still dreaming about becoming an overnight millionaire, first thing to do is: wake up.

But hey, that doesn't mean that you cannot make a living with an online activity if you put in enough effort and time.

Jeff Bezos, the founder of Amazon, didn't create his multibillion dollar business in a couple of months. Actually, he wrote the business plan for Amazon in 1994. And I still remember, reading numerous articles in '95 and the following years, how difficult it was to convince his investors to stick to it, despite the millions of dollars that were pumped in his 'silly' idea, to sell books on the internet. But he stuck to it for years. And see what has become of it. 20 years later it is the biggest online retailer.

What you also won't find in this book, are completely new and interesting ideas for a new startup. Something like 'selling land on the moon' (Actually someone has already done that). Or 'create a startup that will mass-produce high quality 3D printers for $100'. It is perhaps an interesting idea, but out of the scope of this book.

Who is this book intended for?

You may find some useful information in this book if you are in one of the following situations:

-You have a job, but you have difficulties every end of the month, and you are looking for a way to earn some extra money, using your computer at home. This may apply to mums at home, students etc.

-You have a job, but you don't like it and you want to replace your current job with an activity online. AND you want to create a fulltime income out of it. That's totally feasible. Lots of people have done that before you. And if you are prepared to put in enough hours, day after day, you finally may get to your objective.

-You are out of a job, and for whatever reason, you don't want to look for another 9-5 job in the corporate world. You want to become part of this 'online community' and you want to create a fulltime income with it. Now I have to pull a warning flag here. Creating a fulltime income online, is long and hard work. Actually, when you will start to track your hours, against the money you will make, you will find that in the first months, if not years, your hourly wage will not even get close to what you can earn with a 9-5 job. So think carefully before you jump in.

-In all situations, you want to do this either on your own, or maybe with your partner. And over time, maybe outsource some of the work.

To resume, you have not a clear idea what kind of online opportunities exist and how/where to get started. And you want to keep this small; at least in the beginning.

If your intention is to create a second Amazon, I'm afraid you won't find any useful information here. Similar, if you are a seasoned internet marketer with a mailing list of 200.000 subscribers, I don't think you will find any mind-blowing ideas.

How big is the internet business?

Here are some stats about the internet.

INTERNET USAGE STATISTICS
The Internet Big Picture
World Internet Users and 2021 Population Stats

World Regions	Population (2021 Est.)	Population % of World	Internet Users 31 Mar 2021	Penetration Rate (% Pop.)	Growth 2000-2021	Internet World %
Asia	4,327,333,821	54.9 %	2,762,187,516	63.8 %	2,316.5 %	53.4 %
Europe	835,817,920	10.6 %	736,995,638	88.2 %	601.3 %	14.3 %
Africa	1,373,486,514	17.4 %	594,008,009	43.2 %	13,058 %	11.5 %
Latin America / Carib.	659,743,522	8.4 %	498,437,116	75.6 %	2,658.5 %	9.6 %
North America	370,322,393	4.7 %	347,916,627	93.9 %	221.9 %	6.7 %
Middle East	265,587,661	3.4 %	198,850,130	74.9 %	5,953.6 %	3.9 %
Oceania / Australia	43,473,756	0.6 %	30,385,571	69.9 %	298.7 %	0.6 %
WORLD TOTAL	7,875,765,587	100.0 %	5,168,780,607	65.6 %	1,331.9 %	100.0 %

WORLD INTERNET USAGE AND POPULATION STATISTICS — 2021 Year-Q1 Estimates

NOTES: (1) Internet Usage and World Population Statistics estimates are for March 31, 2021. (2) CLICK on each world region name for detailed regional usage information. (3) Demographic (Population) numbers are based on data from the United Nations Population Division. (4) Internet usage information comes from data published by Nielsen Online, by the International Telecommunications Union, by GfK, by local ICT Regulators and other reliable sources. (5) For definitions, navigation help and disclaimers, please refer to the Website Surfing Guide. (6) The information from this website may be cited, giving the due credit and placing a link back to www.internetworldstats.com. Copyright © 2021, Miniwatts Marketing Group. All rights reserved worldwide.

As you can see, the internet is still expanding on a very high rate. And the world wide penetration is 'only' 65%. Sure, there are huge differences between for example Africa and North America. But in total, we are talking about 5.6 billion users! Imagine if you could attract a very tiny percentage, something like 0,001% to your offers. That are 56.000 people !!

Why are people so interested by making money online?

Personally I think that for a good part, this is caused by the 'ideal job' image that is created around these kinds of businesses. Some people call it, the 'internet life-style'. Work wherever you want, whenever you want, and make thousands of dollars a month, just by sitting a couple of hours behind your computer.

Now, I do know people who are making a significant amount of money online, but they achieved that with very hard work. Actually, especially in the beginning, the hours that you have to put in will probably be twice as much as a standard 9 to 5 job.

And let's talk about the other aspects. 'Wherever you want'. For most of the small online businesses, this means in practice: on your own, doors closed, in your home office or on your kitchen table. So if you are a very social minded person who loves to chat for an hour with colleagues at the coffee machine, you will miss this kind of social activity.

'Whenever you want'. In practice, this means at least 8 hours a day, if your long term objective is to create a fulltime income. Sure, you have more flexibility in your working hours. Instead of working Monday to Friday you can decide to work from Saturday till Wednesday. And if you prefer to work at night, you can work from 9:00 pm till 9:00 am. But whatever way you turn it, you have to put in the hours to get there. No shortcuts here.

'And make thousands of dollars a month'. Sure. Yes. Possible. I know people who make anywhere from $20.000 till $100.000 per month and more. Every month. But it took them several years of determination, consistency, continuous learning and trial and error to get there. If you have what it takes, you can also get there although neither over next month nor the year after. Set yourself realistic goals that are achievable.

Now that we have set the scene, let's get to the meat....

Section 1 : Get Paid for tasks on internet

In this section, I will talk about all kinds of things that you can do on the internet, and that can make you some money. Now let's be honest. Whatever you try and regardless of how many hours you put in to these activities, you will never be able to make a fulltime income with these. You can earn some bucks left and right, win coupons, prizes, some free gas etc. A good part of these activities are things that people are doing anyway already on their computer; searching on Google, reading emails, playing games. So instead of spending 2 hours a day on your Facebook, you could have a look at these activities and turn these activities into hard cash!

Take paid surveys

1. www.cashcrate.com : On this site, you can earn a bit of cash in lots of different ways. Try new products, filling out research surveys, shopping, referrals, socializing, and playing games. Payouts vary from a couple of cents to 1000$, depending on your time and efforts.

    The most well-known way of making money with Cashgate is by participating in free offers. These offers are supported by advertisers and let you earn free cash by requesting information from a variety of products and services. For more details check out their complete guide on

2. https://us.toluna.com/ lets you pick the topics you'd like to take surveys. Although this may make the platform more interesting, the payment opportunities aren't that impressive. For each survey, you will earn between 15 and 50,000 points. You may not see the points credited to your account for several days. Unfortunately, your points will expire after being in your account for 12 months. With that, it's important to spend your points relatively quickly. As you redeem points, you will be able to choose from cash via PayPal and several gift card options.

3. Dollar survey. www.dollarsurveys.net . Take a quick survey and earn $1 via PayPal. You can take several surveys every day. Paid already out over 2 million dollars in rewards.

4. https://surveys.gobranded.com/ Branded Surveys is one of the world's leading market research communities - rewarding you for your opinion

5. I-say : www.ipsosisay.com . Sign up for a free account. You can win cash, gift cards and donations.

6. Clear voice surveys :http://www.clearvoicesurveys.com. Get paid to take real surveys from market research companies.

7. Ipoll : www.ipoll.com . Get paid to tell what you think about their products. $5 signup bonus. You can take these surveys anywhere because they work also on mobile. Thus you can earn some cash when sitting in your office or on the beach.

8. https://www.oneopinion.com/This site is a survey aggregator with an effective screening process. Its dashboard is informative and displays helpful sections, such as your activity and a customer support form. The site was above average at picking surveys we qualified

for. As for the points awarded per survey, 500 or 1,000 points may look high at first, but when converted to actual rewards, you'd get 50 cents or a dollar. Also, you can't cash out until you reach 25,000 points, equivalent to $25

9. www.onepoll.com Discover the Power of Your Opinion and get rewards for free money, gift cards, cash coupons and vouchers! Have fun and get paid for doing survey

10. https://www.inboxpounds.co.uk/Lots of fun surveys with a minimum cash payout amount of just $5.

11. GlobalTestMarket   : www.globaltestmarket.com . One of the bigger survey sites. This site sends lots of survey invites. But you may only qualify for them 20-30% of them. You can cash out as soon as your account reaches $50.

12. SurveySavvy . www.surveysavvy.com . You can get paid for online surveys and if you bring in friends. You can also install the SavvyConnect software that includes you in behavioral market research while you browse the internet. You can earn $500 if you win the Superstar contest entry.

13. https://yougov.co.uk/ YouGov is one of the more interesting sites to sign up to because of the kinds of surveys they conduct. Most are on

current issues that are in the news and they encourage you to express your views. Surveys can take up to 30 minutes but are not always that frequent. We received one or two a fortnight, so it can take a few months to hit the threshold. However, you get £1 just for joining and if you get your friends to sign up too you can quickly get lots more points and cash!

14. Opinion Outpost : www.opinionoutpost.com : Take online surveys about electronics, medicine, politics, sports, advertisements, appliances or even what you eat for breakfast. You can earn points and redeem them for cash and other great rewards. Every quarter a winner will receive $10.000 !

Get paid to read emails

Are you buried every day in emails? Everyone who has an internet connection also has an email. Some people spend an hour a week on their emails, and others several hours a day. Now, if there is an activity that is done by millions of people around the world, every day, you can be sure that some clever guys figure out a way to make money with it. So, they invented the activity 'get paid for reading emails'. Yes, it does exist. And no, you will not become a second Donald Trump with it. Most paid emails pay just a few cents.

How does it work? They send you an email that is basically an ad, which promotes a product or a service. Sometimes even with a discount or coupon code. You click on the link in the email and your account gets credited for a few cents regardless of whether you bought something or not. You are paid just for clicking on the link.

Most of these sites also reward you for all kind of other activities. See the next section on GPT (Get Paid To) sites.

15. www.inboxdollars.com : One of the most well-known sites. Signup is free. You get paid out as soon as your account reaches 30$

16. www.sendearnings.com : Very similar to inboxdollars. You even get a 5$ signup bonus. Signup is of course free.

17. www.mypoints.com : This site is very popular among work-from home moms. There are lots of ways to earn points that can be converted either into cash or exchanged for gift cards from dozens of stores.

18. www.inboxpays.com : Here you can earn cash by reading emails. They also have a referral program. You can earn up to $50 per offer. $5 signup bonus.

19. www.upworkptr.com . Get paid for reading emails and clicking banners. Free signup. Paid emails worth $25. $10 for every referral.

Online reward sites

There are lots of sites that reward you with cash back and points, very similar to credit card companies. But unlike the credit card companies you can earn points in lots of different ways: playing games, signing up for a newsletter, visiting websites etc. These sites are called GPT sites (Get Paid To).

Just a word of warning here. These types of sites have been known for being good hunting fields for online scammers. You do all the activities/tasks, they get paid from their advertisers, but when it comes to paying you, they don't. So do your due diligence before signing up for these types of sites.

Having said this, there are luckily some trustworthy sites that will actually pay you for completing offers and shopping.

20. One the most well-known sites in this category is www.swagbucks.com . Here you can earn rewards and free stuff by searching and shopping online, answering surveys. They paid out almost 60 million dollars to their members. Signup is free. You will earn 'swagbucks' which can be exchanged for gifts and prizes like amazon gift cards.

21. Quickrewards.net is also a site where you can earn money in several ways. Doing surveys, visiting websites, shopping, playing games and watching videos. They have redemption offers from WalMart, Amazon, Applebees, Disney etc. The big appeal of this site is, that they payout quickly .

22. www.creationsrewards.net is an online rewards program where you are rewarded for shopping, taking surveys, watching videos, product trials and more. They have literally thousands of coupons & deals. They have a special bonus page where you can earn even more points. It's a real fun site.

Get paid to surf the web

23. cashsurfers : www.cashsurfers.com. Sign up, start surfing the offers. Complete enough deals to earn at least $20. Refer your friends and get 10% of every special offer they complete. Get paid into your PayPal account.

Review Products

Lots of companies want to know what you, the consumer, thinks about their products. The look, the packaging, the price, the taste. To figure that out, they are prepared to send these products to you, so that you test them for them and fill out a survey. Numerous sites propose you to review their products. Here are some of them

24. https://www.univoxcommunity.com/. You can earn from $5 to $75. You may keep the products that you review. They already paid out 2.6 million dollars !

25. Review stream. www.reviewstream.com . On this site you can test all kinds of things and get paid for it. Anti-wrinkle solutions, acne treatments, cellulite treatments, diapers, weight loss supplements. The best reviewer of the year can earn a $2000 bonus. You can earn $5 per review. Minimum payout is $30 through PayPal.

26. Review me. www.reviewme.com . This site is great for bloggers who review products. Submit your site for inclusion on the reviewme network. If approved, your site will enter the reviewme marketplace and clients will purchase reviews from you.

You decide to accept the review or not. You

will be paid $20 to $200 for each completed review that you post on your site.

27. https://www.productreportcard.com/Content is, and will be, the lifeblood of the internet. New and experienced content creators have been frustrated with the tools that are available to ensure their content is both engaging and viral. 18.000 subscribers. For every review you submit you can earn coins. You can make $5 per review.

28. Sponsored Reviews : This one is very similar to ReviewMe. Advertisers and bloggers meet each other here. You can earn cash by writing honest posts about advertiser's products and services. You can also get paid to blog. There are two ways to participate

-You can create a profile for your blog(s) in order to attract advertisers. Advertisers will purchase posts from you directly through this marketplace, which you have the option to accept or decline within 3 days.

-You can also search for advertisers directly, and bid on jobs. Their unique bidding system allows you to negotiate your rates with advertisers in order to maximize your earnings.

Note that there are minimum requirements to participate. (nr of backlinks, number of words on your blog, at least 3 months old, etc.)

Get paid to answer questions

Are you an expert in some field? Do you have specific skills? Do you like helping people and answering their questions? Then these are for you. Answer questions and get paid. You won't make a fortune with it, but you can really help out other people with their questions.

29. www.smallbizadvice.com . As the name suggests, here you can answer questions from small business owners. These can be simple advice, gathering data, how-to information or compiling a complete research report. You pick yourself which topics you want to answer on. The process is rather straight forward: register, bid to answer questions or complete projects. Complete the tasks. And get paid.

30. Are you into psychic mediums, tarot and spiritual readings? Then check out www.keen.com . Sign up as a medium; specify your specialty and rates. You get paid when people consult you online.

31. Bitwine. psychic.bitwine.com . You can setup an account on this site if you can help people with psychological problems. You can become an

advisor in astrology, love guidance, meditation, psychic medium & healing, reiki, spiritual coaching, tarot etc.

32. www.justanswer.com . If you are a legal expert then you can sign up and start answering questions about laws, divorces and other legal issues. And get paid for it.

33. Become a juror. www.ejury.com . eJury provides an attorney the opportunity to "pre-try" the case before it goes to trial in front of an actual jury at the courthouse. Cases at the courthouse are usually tried to juries of 12 people. At eJury, each case is tied to a minimum of 50 people. For every verdict rendered you can earn $5-$10. You certainly will not get rich with this one.

34. Chegg. www.chegg.com (formerly StudentOfFortune). If you are a student and want to help other students in your field of expertise, you can earn some money here. You can also sell your study books. 5 million students on over 7000 campuses.

35. Tutor. www.tutor.com . If you like teaching you can use your skills on this site and make a part-time income as a tutor in accounting, economics, finance, physics and more. You can make anywhere between $800 and $1600 a month.

Get paid to search on search engines

36. Bing rewards : Join http://www.bing.com/explore/rewards and get rewarded for searching and working with Bing. You can earn gift cards, Microsoft points for Xbox, movie nights from Redbox and more.

37. Become a Google rater : Google has a legitimate work at home opportunity in the form of its ads quality rater. These are often bilingual jobs. The tasks consist of analyzing and providing feedback on text, web pages, and search results. Other companies hire for similar jobs which they call internet assess or search evaluators. To become a Google rater you have to go to http://www.google.com/about/jobs/ and search for 'rater'.

Get paid to listen to music

38. Get paid to listen to Music : https://www.hitpredictor.com/. Sign up and music will arrive in your inbox, depending on what type of music you prefer. Sit back and listen. And get paid a little.

39. In the same category, you can also go to https://playlistpush.com/. If you are a content creator with a good number of people following you, PlaylistPush is a great platform to make some extra cash. To get started, you should have at least 400 followers on Apple Music or Spotify. Once you meet this requirement, you will be able to connect with new artists who pay popular users to listen to their music and add them to their own playlists

Get paid to read ads

40. Get paid to read ads : Signup for free at https://home.ibotta.com/. You can earn cash instantly online, in-store and on the go with participating brands. You'll also receive personalized cash back offers when you shop with Ibotta. Watch videos, give feedback and earn instant cash. Or click on the Ibotta logo on any of the partners' sites. That ad pays you also. Share it on Faceook, Twitter and Pinterest with your friends. If they join Ibotta, your weekly earn limit will even increase more.

Get paid to socialize

41. https://rentafriend.com/ Rent a Friend is a legit site that does exactly what it says in its name, in that it lets you rent someone to be your friend. In particular, it emphasizes that its services are purely platonic. It's mostly focused on in-person meet ups but they do allow you to limit yourself to being a virtual friend, so you'll only talk online with people. They really emphasize letting clients know in your profile if you have a special skill, as a lot of people use the site as a way to not only meet someone new, but to learn something. This can be anything from speaking Spanish to being good at baking to being really into astrology. Whatever your thing is, let people know as who knows who else is interested in learning about it.

42. https://www.rentacyberfriend.com/ Rent a Cyber Friend is pretty similar to Rent a Friend except that, as you may have figured out from its name, it's purely for people who want to get paid to be a virtual friend. To join, you simply build your profile which involves listing your location, some interests and how you want to chat. On that last point, it can include things like Facebook Messenger, Skype, WhatsApp and more. You can take a look at some of the other potential friends on there without signing up, so it's worth checking out the site before signing up to see the kind of information you'd provide as a potential   friend   too.

43. https://www.friendpc.com/ FriendPC is another good option if you're looking to get paid to be an online friend for someone. It offers all the options for talking with your new friend that you could possibly think of – text message, chat room, phone call, online call...whatever works for you is likely an option here. Users have to pay a small fee to request to talk to you, which helps to make sure that the people who approach you really do want to chat. The site also emphasizes that it's not only for people who just want to be friends, but also those looking to learn a new skill or even get a life coach. So if they sound like something you'd be able to provide, perhaps look into FriendPC to earn a bit of cash.

Get paid to upload and share files

You can make money by uploading files to file sharing hosting companies. Some of them will offer a premium account to their uploaders and others will reward you with hard cash. You can upload photos, wallpapers, songs, programs etc.

You will get paid, depending on the number of times your files get downloaded. Notice that this is a bit grey area, because a certain number of these sites, like hotfile and megaupload and others have been closed down because they were sharing all kinds of copyrighted material. Movies, albums etc.

So, be careful if you want to try this, and what you upload and share. Here are some sites that operate in the paid file sharing space :

44.   https://rapidgator.net/ Rapidgator is a popular file hosting website that allows users to upload their files and share them with the audience. The more people download your file, the more money comes into your pocket. There are three uploading methods such as FTP, remote upload, and web upload. They have two models for uploaders to make money. You can

either choose "pay per download" or "pay per sale" to get started with money making with Rapidgator.

45.   https://www.file-upload.com/ File Upload is a cloud file storage service that pays users when their files get downloaded. Users can make from $2 to $7 for a thousand downloads, depending upon the tier and file size. File Upload is one of those companies that pay out through various payment solutions such as Skrill, Payoneer, PayPal, Western Union, Neteller, Bitcoin, Ethereum, MoneyGram, and more. This service gives an immense opportunity to make some extra money with blogging..

46.   https://www.indishare.org/ Indishare is a file hosting website that pays for every 10,000 downloads. They pay between $2 to $10 for different file sizes across four tiers. The minimum payout is $10, which can be received after one month. They process payouts on every 20th. However, what differentiates Indishare from other file hosting services is that they pay for 10,000 downloads instead of 1,000 downloads

Get paid to tweet

Yes, you can make money by sending tweets on twitter. Now let's be honest. You will not going to make any significant money if you tweet to your couple of hundred followers.

But if you happen to have a followers list that runs into tens of thousands then this can become an easy way to make money.

Companies are starting to realize that even a tweet from an average user to his friends can have more effect then a paid ad on a site. This is similar to the famous word-of-mouth.

47. SponsoredTweets : www.sponsoredtweets.com. One of the biggest sites in its category where famous people get paid to tweet. But even with a couple of hundred followers you can make some bucks.

48. Thenetworkniche . https://www.thenetworkniche.com/get-paid-to-tweet/. On this site, even an average twitter user can earn up to $5 per tweet.

49. Manage a Twitter account for a client. You'd be amazed at how many brands and businesses are intimidated by sending 140 characters into the Twitterverse. You can manage their Twitter account by scheduling tweets ahead of time with Hootsuite.com for the brand or business to approve them before they're sent.

Get paid to play games

50. www.cashdazzle.com is one of the largest casual gaming communities. You can earn tokens to play their games and win cash prizes. The games are easy to play and fun to discover. All the games are games of chance, so the more you play, the more likely you are to win.

Get paid to click

Pay-to-Click sites (PTC), are sites where you get paid by clicking on ads. I have included these just to be as complete as possible. But beware that this is also a well-know playfield for scammers. You spend time to click on ads, but you never will get paid. And honestly, it really brings in cents. But I'll mention two that seem to be trustworthy.

51. www.neobux.com . As a member, you can earn money just by watching ads. Your points can be redeemed for prizes. If you get new referrals in, you will also win points on their efforts.

52. www.clixsense.com . This site will pay you for visiting sites, doing micro tasks, playing ClixGrid. They also have a referral program. You can install a browser toolbar to get instant notification of new ads available. 3 million members. You can earn $ 0,02 per click. You can do the math yourself...

Section 2 : Affiliate Marketing

When I started this section, I hesitated to name it 'Affiliate Marketing'. Because for people that are completely new to online business this may sound like a strange word. So for a moment, I thought about calling it 'become an online salesman '(or woman) . Because that's what affiliate marketing is all about.

Therefore, before going a bit further into how you can make money with affiliate marketing , I think I need to explain a bit more in detail what affiliate marketing is and how things fit together. Notice that this book is not 'the complete guide to affiliate marketing'. The subject on its own may well require another book of several hundreds of pages. Because affiliate marketing is a vast subject.

So, what is affiliate marketing? Let's go back the offline (or real) world. In the offline world, you could decide to become a salesman for, let's say an insurance company. And purely commission based. Which means : No sales, no money.

You sign a simple contract with insurance company A , and start selling their products. How do you go about this? That depends a lot on your personal profile. If you have been in the insurance world for already two decades, it might be enough to open your address book and start making phone calls. Or you might decide to place an ad in the local newspaper and wait for the calls. Or you might decide to go from door to door, or cold calling.

You see, there are lots of different ways to find potential customers. Finally, when you have found a potential customer, and you have sold a product to them, the insurance company will pay you a commission. Sounds simple. Well, on paper it is. In real life it requires effort and time to get there.

Nothing prevents you from working for a second, different, insurance company B. You sign up another contract, and when you visit your potential customers, you can now offer products from two companies.

Now let's get back to the online world and see how this works out. There are lots of people and companies that create products and services. Software, eBooks, online courses, dating sites, etc. To sell them, they have two solutions :

Either they sell it themselves, or they hire affiliates (=online salesman) to sell their products and services or both. Notice that I say 'hire', but it isn't really hiring. You, the affiliate, chooses which product you want to sell. IF, and only IF you make a sale, you get a commission.

You can become an affiliate for 2, 3, 5 or 10 different companies. And you start already to see the potential problem you will be running in. You will have to do the accounting for 10 different companies. Sign 10 different contracts etc. Collect your commissions from 10 different offices.

On the other hand, when you look at it from the sellers' side, for them, setting up an affiliate program is an investment in time and money. They have to keep track of their affiliates, the sales of every affiliate, payout the commissions to hundreds or sometimes thousands of affiliates. In short, this can become quickly a major headache for a small company.

This is where affiliate sites get into play. They act as an intermediate, or broker, between on one hand, people who have to sell something and on the other hand affiliates who are prepared to spend time and effort to find customers for these products or services.

It's a pretty good win-win situation. Assume you're a programmer and you have developed a great piece of software. Now, developing it is one thing, selling it is another. So how do you go about this? You can setup your account as a seller on an affiliate network. The sellers (affiliates) of this network may choose your product to promote it, because they have some infinity with your product, or they have tried it and really think that it is a great piece of software.

When you make a sale for let's say $100 for this software, the developer might decide to give you 50%. The network that sits in between the software developer and the affiliate (=you), will also take of a percentage to cover their costs and make a profit. Let's say 10%. The developer will finally get 40% on the sale.

Now, not every company that has something to sell will work through an intermediate broker or affiliate network. They will do all the affiliate administration themselves.

Here you are. That's what, in a nutshell, affiliate marketing is all about.

Do you need a website to do affiliate marketing?

Let's go back to our salesman that I mentioned before. Does he need a car? If he uses his address book with hundreds of contacts and does everything over the phone, strictly speaking he doesn't need a car.

But if he wants to do door-to-door sales, yes, then he needs a car.

The same applies to affiliate marketing. Strictly speaking, no, you don't need a website. The key question is : **How** are you going to find potential customers?

Somehow you have to get your message under the eyeballs of your buyers. Now there are several ways where you can find potential customers. And not all of them require a website. For example, you could just write about your product(s) on your Facebook.

And there are article sites, where you can post your articles for free. And you can create a free blog.

But let's be honest. If you don't have a website, it will be much more difficult to attract people to your products.

How do you get traffic?

We're actually getting into one of the key questions: How do you generate traffic to your offerings? With or without your own website. Now, that on itself is again a huge subject, and out of the scope of this book. But let me give you some pointers in the right direction. There are basically two ways to generate traffic :

-Free traffic

-Paid traffic

Free traffic

There are numerous ways to get free traffic. But as usual, free will only get you as far as what you can aspect from something free. It's like a logo design program, that will allow you to create a wonderful logo, but the free version of the program doesn't allow you to save it. Or a free trial version that times out after a week. Good to test the waters, but over time you might have to consider the paid traffic. But nothing prevents you to start off with the free possibilities and, when you have made some small amount of money, put something back into paid traffic.

Notice that there isn't ONE way of doing affiliate marketing. Or the best way. The only thing that will be important for you is, if YOUR way is going to work.

In that sense, it is not very different from sales in the offline world. To sell something or to attract customers, you can do all kinds of things :

-Put an advertisement in front of your shop

-Put an advertisement in the local newspaper

-Get onto the yellow pages

-Make an ad on the radio

-Get an article in the local newspaper.

-Put in place a loyalty program

And the same holds for our insurance salesman. Some people are excellent in this, and can make a sale over the phone, and might achieve a result of 10% successful calls. And other people, who are not so gifted with sales skills, will maybe only make 1 sale on every 100 door-to-door visits.

A lot depends on how much time you want to put in your online activity. And how much money you intend to make with your efforts. But let me tell you immediately the hard truth. If you spend 1 or 2 hours a day on whatever online activity you undertake, it will be very unlikely that you can make a living out of it. It is just too much work. But if your objective is to earn just a couple of hundred bucks a month, and you are prepared to stick with your 1 or 2 hour a day for a long period, then you finally will get there.

This book is not 'a complete guide to traffic'. But let me summarize in a short list how you can generate traffic to your site:

-Use content revenue sharing sites like squidoo, hubpages etc. (see the separate chapter on 'content revenue sharing'

-Answer posts in forums that are related to your niche

-Make guest posts on blogs which operate in the same niche as yours.

Paid traffic

As stated before, the subject of 'how to get paid traffic to your site/products' is a very fast subject, which would require another book. But for completeness, I will include a list of things you can do to get traffic to your site and products.

-You can use Facebook ads. They are extremely cheap

-Get a Google Adwords account and setup your paid ads on Adwords

-Buy soloads. How does this work? You go to a site where people buy and sell ads. You buy a certain quantity of ads from a seller. The seller will send email ads to his email list with your message. When a potential customer opens their email and clicks on the link(s) in the email, they get redirected to your site. You probably may have understood that if you have a significant email list yourself, you can make substantial money out of this with soloads. Here are some places where you can go for solo ads.

-www.monstersoloads.com

www.rent-a-list.com-

-www.premiumsolos.com

-www.soloadsx.com

CPA networks.

In addition to the traditional networks, there also exists what's called CPA networks. CPA stands for Cost-per-Action. A CPA network talks about 'Advertisers' and 'Publishers'. An advertiser goes to a CPA network to promote his products. You, as a publisher, will promote these products.

Affiliate programs

Now that we have cleared up what affiliate marketing is about let's have a look in detail how and where you can make money with this.

53. Amazon affiliate program. This is the affiliate program created by Amazon. They call it Amazon Associates. Go to https://affiliate-program.amazon.com and sign up for free. How does it work?

Suppose you have a site on fitness equipment. On that site you talk about different fitness machines, you do reviews and more. People who are looking to buy a treadmill might fall on your site, because you have written an in depth article about treadmills. Now what would be more logical then putting up an ad just next to the text, or into the article where you sell a $5000 treadmill?

I hear you say : 'But I don't have a treadmill for sale!'. And that's where the beauty of Amazon associates comes into play. Before putting up your ad, you go to amazon and you look for treadmills that they sell. You just copy the link to that product on your page with the amazon ad, and magically, a complete ad, supplied by amazon with description, photo and price appears on YOUR site.

When your visitor clicks on the treadmill ad, he gets redirected to Amazon. And when that visitor indeed buys that treadmill you get a commission on it! Somewhere between 4% and 8% depending on the total number of products that you sell this way through amazon. Let's say 5% on this sale. That's $250 !!

(for details on their commissions , go to

https://affiliate-program.amazon.com/gp/associates/help/operating/advertisingfees)

And all the rest? Shipping the machine, transport, duties, taxes, guarantee? That's all taken care of by amazon! As soon as the customer clicks the buy button, your work is finished and you get your commission.

A certain portion of affiliate marketers consider that the commissions from Amazon are too low. And indeed, percentage wise they are, compared for example with Clickbank (we'll get there later).

But this disadvantage is partially compensated by two major advantages :

1. Amazon is a real war machine when it comes down to making retail sales on the internet. The smartest marketers and the

best programmers have spent now 20 years to get there. Everything is extremely optimized. You may not have noticed, but if you're a regular Amazon customer, notice everything that happens on your screen. You see items that you have bought, items that you have looked at, sometimes even a year ago. They show you items which are similar to the ones you are looking for etc.etc. In short, when you get a customer to their site, there is a pretty good chance that this customer will buy something.

2. As a consequence of the previous, Amazon does a particularly good job into up selling. What's that? An up sell is when someone buys let's say a pair of skis, which was what he actually was looking for. But immediately when the customer is presented with the description of the pair of skis, Amazon shows him also all kinds of related products. Ski gloves, Ski helmets, goggles, ski boots, ski bags etc.etc.

3. And there is a good chance that the customer buys another one or two of these items. And the beauty is : You will also get a commission on these additional products sold !!

Now let's do the math again. Suppose that you have a site about skiing. 'How to learn to ski', or 'where to ski' or whatever. And suppose that the customer came to Amazon because you have an ad on your site for $500 rossignol skis. Normally you would have expected let's say 5% or 25$ commission on this.

But the same customer also buys : a pair of ski boots for $100 , a $40 goggle, and a $90 ski bag. Total : 500+100+40+90= $730. On which you get 5% or $36.50. If you now calculate it back to the $500 skis that you only advertised, you are actually getting 7,3%.

And let's assume that you just had an ad on your site for the $40 goggle, but the same customer buys through an up sell a $500 pair of skis and all the rest. Now the commission is skyrocketing. The math : Normally you would have expected to get 5% on $40. That's $2. Instead, you get the $36,50 as mentioned before. Result : 91.25%.

54. Ebay partner network (EPN) : https://partnernetwork.ebay.com/ Ebay is the largest auction site on the internet. You can make money by selling your products on this site. We'll get to that later. However, you can also make money by becoming an Ebay partner. In this case, you use affiliate links on your own site, which link to products on Ebay. EPN uses what they call 'Quality Click Pricing'.

Affiliates are paid based on an algorithm that measures several factors like revenue from sales, long term value of new users, etc.

To become an Ebay Partner, you have to apply for it. And your application will only be accepted if you have enough quality traffic to your site.

Other affiliate sites

The following sites are all affiliate networks as described before. Sellers go there to sell an affiliate product (or service). And affiliate marketers go there to find products to sell.

55. Clickbank. www.clickbank.com . Ask an affiliate marketer to name an affiliate site and they probably will say Clickbank. Clickbank has mostly Digital products. Courses, eBooks, software etc. Created in 1998. Signing up as an affiliate is free.

At the moment of this writing they have over 100.000 different products to promote. Go to 'marketplace' and browse through the different categories.

Here is an example of a product :

Tedswoodworking 16,000 Plans - $125 Per Sale ~1 In 11 Conversions! (view mobile)
New Sales Video Triples Conversion Rates! Earn Up To $125 Per Sale With Multiple Upsells. We Have The Highest Conversions & Payouts Vs Other Offers With The Lowest Refunds. The Original Woodworking Site On Cb. Aff Tools At: Http://tedswoodworking.com/aff

Avg $/sale
$59.90

PROMOTE

Vendor Spotlight

Stats: Initial $/sale: $59.84 | Avg %/sale: 75.0% | Avg Rebill Total: $53.85 | Avg %/rebill: 75.0% | Grav: 163.46
Cat: Home & Garden : Crafts & Hobbies

When you promote this product and you make a sale, you will earn on average $59.90. See that small blue icon at the bottom? That means that this product has recurring revenue.

When a customer signs up for this product, he will be billed on a monthly basis. And you will get a part of that every month. Commission rates vary but are typically 50% and this can go up to 70%. This percentage is determined by the seller when he sets up his product.

When selecting products from clickbank, also watch the Gravity. (Grav); in this case, 163.46. Gravity gives an indication about the competition that there is on this product. A gravity of 0 means : no competition. The higher the gravity, the more competition there is.

You might be tempted to take products with zero gravity because there is no competition. But if there is no competition it probably means that this product is not selling. Having competition, with a high gravity, means that the product sells. I would recommend considering only products that have as a minimum a gravity of 10-15.

To promote a product, just click on the 'promote' button and you will get a 'hoplink'. Paste that link onto a webpage on your site, into a mail, on your FB and you're all set.

There's much more to say about clickbank, hoplinks and how to choose a product, but that's out of the scope of this book.

56.   Commission Junction. Or actually 'CJ Affiliate by Conversant'. https://www.cj.com/ . In the way it functions, it is a lot similar to clickbank. But they have also real products (not only digital products). Electronics, clothes, computers, books. Etc.

You need to have a website to apply. And you need to have already visitors. Only apply for an account when you have already an established site with a specific target audience. Full details what you need to join are here https://www.cj.com/publisher/join

57. Shareasale : www.shareasale.com . Another affiliate network site. Created in 2000. All kind of products. Digital and physical. Home & garden, fashion, decoration, crafts. Over 2000 merchants to select products from. Commissions depend on the products you promote, but are typically around 10%. They provide tools to make a video. They also have a 'Make-a-Page' feature.

58. Linkshare . www.linkshare.com . Hundreds of advertisers in multiple categories. You have to apply, and advertisers will check your site and accept you as an affiliate or not. They also have 'open' programs, which means that the advertisers will automatically accept you as an affiliate.

59. Neverblue.com. www.neverblue.com . Free to join. But they will not accept all applications. Affiliate tools like Banner rotator, Pixel manager. They have the reputation that they pay out accurately and timely. Very good tools for advanced tracking and monitoring your traffic.

60. MaxBounty. www.maxbounty.com . Max bounty is among the best CPA networks to earn money and it is highly recommended by most internet marketers and affiliates. The signup process is easy and fast. Easy to use interface. Minimum payout is $50.

61. Clixgalore www.clixgalore.com . They have an 'Instant web site builder' tool. This allows you to create easily promotional web pages.

62. AdscendMedia . www.adscendmedia.com . AdscendMedia is a CPA marketing solution dedicated to providing high quality leads to advertisers and great payouts and services to affiliates. The network is a great option because it provides and pays per click marketing strategy therefore making it a cheap option. Over 2000 offers. Minimum payout is $50. You have to apply and most people attempting for the first time get rejected.

63. CPAlead. www.cpalead.com . Created in 2006. One of the top 10 CPA networks. They have a Content Gateway tool which comes between the content of your site and the visitor. When the visitor fills in a survey, you get a commission. $50 minimum payout. More than 2000 offers . Only to be considered if you have a high traffic website.

64. Peerfly : www.peerfly.com. 30000 active publishers in 165 countries. No monthly Fees. Offers one of the most lucrative types of commissions. Minimum payout $50.

65. Clickbooth www.clickbooth.com . Over 3000 advertisers. Minimum payout $50. A wide range of offerings across different niches. For advanced affiliates, because it may take a long time before you get accepted into the network.

66. Convert2Media : www.convert2media.com. Another leading CPA network. Over 1000 advertisers. Minimum payout is $100. 2% referral program.

67. I wasn't sure where to put this one, but if you do affiliate marketing (or any other form of internet marketing) then you seriously should consider building a list. Actually, if I had to give only ONE advice out of this whole book, it would be : start building an email list , right from day one.

How does it work in one sentence : When people visit your site you offer them a freebie . A report, an eBook, a course. You give away the freebie in exchange for their email. When you grow your list to thousands of subscribers, you can sell to them over and over again.

Section 3 : Sell your products

Do you create your own products? Craftswork, photos, paintings, clothes? Whatever you create yourself, you can very likely sell it somewhere on internet. This section covers a number of ways what, how and where you can sell your own products.

Sell your images

Are you a good photographer? Do you have high quality pictures on various subjects? Sundowns, landscapes, beaches, animals, buildings? If you do, you sell them on dedicated sites.

68. Shutterpoint : www.shutterpoint.com . 85% payout rate. Payouts by check or Paypal. Minimum payout $50.

69. Bigstockphoto : www.bigstockphoto.com . Over 17 million photos. Minimum payout $30. Commissions depend on the size of the photo that a buyer downloads. This can vary from $0.50 up to several dollars per image.

70. Istockphoto. www.istockphoto.com . One of the biggest stock photo sites. You can contribute photos, videos, audio and illustrations. Minimum payout $100. You get 20% of the total price for mages between $1 and $20.

71. Fotolia : www.fotolia.com . 27 millions photos. Royalty payouts vary from 20% to 63%.

72. Shutterstock : www.shutterstock.com . 20 million images. You can sell photos, vector/illustrations (EPS files) and videos.

73. Thinkstock . www.thinkstockphotos.com . This site belongs to 'Getty Images'. The same group that owns istockphoto.

74. DreamsTime : www.dreamstime.com . Sell your photos and get 25%-60% on every sale. Over 22 million photos.

75. CreStock. www.crestock.com Royalties payout vary from 20% to 40% . The more you sell, the higher the payout per photo. Minimum payout is $50.

76. PhotoStockPlus : www.photostockplus.com . One of the highest paying stock sites. Royalties can go up to 85%. You can set your own prices.

77. 123RoyaltyFree. www.123rf.com . 26 million photos. You get 50% of each photo you sell. You earn a 15% referral fee plus 10% of every image sold by a photographer you refer.

Selling your own products.

If you create your own products, here are a couple of sites where you can sell your creations.

78. Amazon www.amazon.com. The biggest retail site in the world. Hundreds of categories and subcategories. No per-item listing fee. They have separate programs for professional and individual sellers. You make your own listing, upload it to amazon. When customers buy your product, you get paid, minus a transaction fee that is charged by amazon. The big advantage of selling on amazon is that it attracts millions of visitors every month.

79. Selling products on Amazon can be very lucrative. The downside of selling physical products is that you have to pack and ship every individual item, go the post office to deliver them etc. When I ran my Ebay business, these tasks were taking up a considerable amount of time.

Amazon has come up with a very nice solution for this. It is called Fulfillment by Amazon (FBA). How does this work? Let's say you find a couple of pallets with products that your local hardware store wants to get rid of, because he needs the space for new products. You buy these pallets of products for 70% or 80% or 90% off.

Now you ship the complete pallets to your nearest Amazon distribution center. You make your listing on Amazon, but when the customer buys your product from Amazon, they will do all the shipping and handling for you. This is actually a very interesting way to make money with products on Amazon, without all the hassle of keeping inventory, packaging, handling. For more details, check out this page http://services.amazon.com/content/fulfillment-by-amazon.htm .

80. Ebay www.ebay.com . The biggest auction site in the world. Here you can sell your products on auction. You set the starting price and let people bid for 5, 7 or 10 days. You can specify also a minimum price, under which you will not sell your product.

You can also sell just by setting a fixed price. As with amazon, the big advantage is that it attracts millions of visitors every month. So you don't have to worry too much on 'how do I get visitors to my products'.

81. Where to find products to sell? When I ran my Ebay business I exclusively bought things at auctions. These are places where you can find very good deals on all kinds of stuff. Cars, wine, telephones, fashion, computers, etc. You can checkout several sites to see if there are auctions in your area :

-www.usauctions.net

-
http://www.treasury.gov/services/Pages/auctions_index.aspx
-Usauctionbrokers.com

82. Another way to sell products on Amazon or Ebay, is by dropshipping. How does this work? You find a supplier for product X. This can be anywhere in the world. US, Europe, China. You make a deal on the buying price for that product. The price will of course depend on how many of the items you will buy.

When you have done this, you can put your product up on Amazon or Ebay. When your product gets sold, your supplier will 'dropship' the item directly to your customer.

The advantage here is, again, that you don't need a depot for storage and you don't have to go through all the hassle of packaging and shipping.

The downside is, that you have little or no-control over the whole shipping process. So if your supplier ships out the products late, you may end up with an angry customer.

If you want to know more about drop shipping, you can find several excellent guides on this on amazon. A good start is

-'The Drop shipping Guide: How to Start Your Drop shipping Business Without the Learning Curve' from Alexander Sinclair

-'How and Where to Locate the Merchandise to Sell on eBay: Insider Information You Need to Know from the Experts Who Do It Every Day' by Dan W. Blacharski.

- E-Commerce Blueprint: The Step-by-Step Guide to Online Store Success'.By Rob Marbry

83. Craigslist. www.craigslist.org . Craigslist is the most well-known site for selling through classified ads. You can sell just about anything here. From furniture to fashion and from cars to electronics. Created in 1995 by Craig Newman. The site has expanded to over 50 countries. **Tip** : If you have nothing to sell, search for giveaways in your area. Search for the word 'giveaway' or search for products with a price between $0.00 and $0,01. Lots of people are putting up stuff that they just want to get rid of. Couches, chairs, tables etc. Put up an ad on one of the other sites (Ebay, Oodle, etc.). When you sell it, you go and pickup the free item.

84. Cafepress. https://www.cafepress.com/. If you have good design skills you can make money here. You create and upload a design. Cafepress sells your design on teacups, T-shirts, pillows, shower curtains etc. Every time that your design is used on a product you earn a commission. Signup is free and it is a rather fun site.

85. Gazelle. www.gazelle.com . This site is specialized in Apple products. iPhones, iPods, Macbooks etc. If you have these items, and you want to get rid of them, you can send them to gazelle. They will give you a quote what they think it is worth and, if you agree, will buy it from you.

86. Oodle : www.oodle.com . A similar site as graigslist, but much smaller. They also have a special section 'Free items', which you can put up for sale on another site.

87. Zazzle : www.zazzle.com . This site is very similar to cafepress. You upload a design. Customers may choose your design which then gets used on clothes, linen, and watches. You can setup your own shop with hundreds of products with your own design.

88. Etsy . www.etsy.com . Etsy is a marketplace for crafters, artists and collectors to sell their handmade creations, vintage goods (at least 20 years old), and both handmade and non-handmade crafting supplies. Of course, you can also sell products to you have purchased from a supplier. $0.20 to list an item. On every sale Etsy takes a 3,5% commission. 30 million buyers. Setting up a shop on Etsy is free.

89. Skreened. https://www.facebook.com/skreened/ Works exactly the same as zazzle or cafepress. Excellent customer service. If you're into T-shirts design, this one is for you.

90. SpreadShirt. www.spreadshirt.com . Create your own T-shirts. You can also sell T-shirts from other designers and earn a commission.

91. PrintFection http://www.printfection.com/ . Create your own, free , T-shirts store, with your own designs.

92. If you have developed a good info product you can sell it as a WSO (Warrior Special Offer) on the warriorforum www.warriorforum.com

93. One of the most profitable ways of making money online is creating a membership site. Sure, this will take a lot of time and effort to get there. You will need to create great content. Update it regularly. Market it. But imagine the income potential if you have a membership site with several hundred or thousand subscribers, who pay you $10 or $20 or $30 dollars, every month. You can do the math...

Section 4 : Sell your services

Freelancing

One of the best ways to earn income from home, using your computer, is through freelancing. All you need is a specific skill, like translating, graphics design, composing music, making logos, eBook covers, fast writing. And if you have good administration skills (editing, emailing, accounting etc.) you can even become a virtual assistant (VA). Here are a couple of ideas where to start if you want to get started as a freelancer.

94. www.odesk.com . This is one of the largest and most well-known site for freelancers. You can setup quickly an account and start to sell your expertise. You can think of web programming, doing SEO, develop software, freelance writing, web design, data entry. You set your own rates. Either an hourly fee or on a fixed-price project.

95. www.microlancer.com . This site was previously known as freelanceswitch. But they merged with Tuts+. The jobs here are more focused on : design, web development, wordpress customization. Icon design, art& illustration, image editing, eBook design. In short, it is more focused on 'technical' jobs. A great site if you're a geek to make some money, or to get something done if your technical skills are limited.

96. www.elance.com . One of the other large freelance sites. This site is really huge. Over 200.000 programmers, 25.000 mobile app developers, 230.000 writers. 50.000 people in marketing. But of course, you can also offer some very special skill like : translating to Hungarian , making a podcast from a document if you have a particular voice.

97. www.freelancer.com : another huge freelance site. You can do logo design, article writing, coding HTML, programming MySQL. Over 10 million users.

98. www.99designs.com : As the name implies, this freelance site is particularly well-known for getting graphics design done. Logos, eBook covers, packaging labels, slogans etc. So, if you're a Photoshop expert or you have good artistic skills you definitely should check out this site to offer your services.

99. www.fiverr.com . This is, in my opinion, by far the most 'fun' site to offer services or getting things done. Every task is called a gig and the standard price is 5$. If things are a bit more complicated, you can charge several gigs (units of 5$) for your task. Now, on this site, you can literally propose almost anything. Play a fake girlfriend for someone, sing a song , make a picture from a famous building in your neighborhood, promote a site by making a picture of yourself in front of the Eiffel tower or another unique place, play a piece of guitar, 'like' someone on Facebook, tweet messages to a jealous boyfriend. Even if you're never going to use this site, just take a look at it, because it is really fun what people propose here.

100. http://jobs.problogger.net . This site is the problogger job board. This is where bloggers looking for jobs and companies looking for bloggers to hire meet. If you are good in blogging, you should definitely have a look at this site.

101. www.peopleperhour.com . Very similar to the previous sites, but not as big. The same principle applies. Setup your profile, specify your skills, and wait for someone that needs your skills to do a specific job, and get paid.

102. www.crowdspring.com : a site with 150.000 creative people from 185 countries. Here you can help people finding a good company name, a slogan, an advertising tag, do info graphics, brochures, design posters, design a complete website (less than 4 pages). Projects start at 299$.

103. www.guru.com : another freelancing site. Over 900.000 'gurus' available to get your job done. And since we are talking about making money, if you are an AutoCAD guru, an iPhone app guru or an SEO guru, you can monetize your skills over here.

104. www.ifreelance.com : Not as big as the other sites, but you can also signup as a freelancer here. You do pay a monthly fee to create a profile and bid on projects. As opposed to the other sites mentioned, ifreelance doesn't charge commissions or transaction fees.

To close this section on freelancing : whatever your skills are, you can propose them online on any of these sites. And of course, nothing prevents you from working on several of these sites. The more work you do, the more ratings you get, the more you move to the top of 'good performers', and the more money you can make.

Microjobs

I have dedicated a special section on what I call 'micro jobs'. These are very simple tasks that can make you some dollars.

105. Mechanical turk. www.mturk.com . This is the most well-known site in this category. Setup by amazon. Tasks are called hits. Tasks can be : tagging pictures, collecting Facebook data, verify captions, search for company information, etc. When you pick up a task, you have to complete it in a predefined time. For every hit you complete, you can earn a couple of cents or a dollar. Some hits can pay up to $50.

106. microworkers. www.microworkers.com . The approach of this site is similar to mechanical turk. 500.000 workers worldwide.

107. ClickChores   :
https://earn-free.ucoz.com/index/earn_with_clickchores/0-21 .

Micro job examples : `

   -FB share my post
   -twitter retweet my tweet
   -comment with this keyword on my blog
   -surf my site and click my +1
   -bookmark me on delicious
   -stumble my site
   -etc.etc.

You get the idea. For every 'micro job' completed you earn a couple of cents. You get paid though PayPal or Payza.

Writing

If you like writing and you can write a lot, you can make money with that skill. One of the ways is to create a blog. If your blog has enough interest, over time, and if you have enough visitors that regularly come back to your blog, you can monetize your blog.

There are several sites where you can create a free blog. However, if you want to make money with a blog I would strongly suggest you to get your own domain name and hosting. This doesn't cost a fortune.

For a couple of dollars a month you can have your own domain name and hosting. With the free blogs you run very quickly into limitations. You cannot install whatever you want, you cannot advertise. However, some people create a free blog just to test the waters. When they have some success with it they move it over to their own domain.

108. You can setup a free blog on www.blogger.com . This the free web publishing tool from Google, for sharing text, photos and video.

109. You can also setup a free blog on www.wordpress.com . It is very easy to create a blog with wordpress.

110. Another free blogging platform is www.livejournal.com . It is not just a blogging platform, but you can also create communities. It is a social networking site.

111. www.tumblr.com is probably one of the most successful blogging sites. Although it is mostly used by personal bloggers, it has gained also some popularity from serious bloggers. They use tumblr to drive traffic to their own site.

You can also write articles for other bloggers. Popular bloggers need consistently new articles. And sometimes, they either have no inspiration or no time or both. And that's where you can come in. If you can write interesting articles, you can make some money with it.

112. www.constant-content.com : Here you can submit **unique** content. 70.000 professional writers submit here their articles and put them for sale. You set the price for your article. You can sell it as 'usage', which means that you maintain the copyright. It's like renting your article out. You can also sell its unique usage. In this case, the buyer becomes the unique owner of the article. And finally you can sell Full Rights. In this case, the buyer becomes the unique owner and he may change and edit it as he pleases. As a guideline, articles sell from 10$ up to 100$ for very specialized articles.

113. www.textbroker.com : Well, the name says it all. You write articles and you put them up for sale. Or you can write an article on demand for someone, given specific keywords, or a specific length. 100.000 authors (US based)

114. Yahoo! Contributor network : https://contributor.yahoo.com/ . Here you can

contribute as many articles, photos and videos you want. You earn money depending on the amount of traffic that your work receives. You can contribute in all kinds of special dedicated websites from Yahoo! News, local, sports, finance, TV, travel, movies, shopping etc.

115. www.cracked.com . You can use this site if you can write funny articles, make fun videos or have the skill to make people laugh. People love funny stuff. For every unique article you can earn up to $100. This site has a vast audience so if your work is really funny, it could attract lots of visitors.

116. www.seekingalpha.com . If you are a crack in stock trading, day trading or other financial topics, then this site is for you. If you are able to write an interesting article they will be happy to pay you for that.

117. The Motley fool (www.fool.com) . Another site with finance information. Stock trading advice, financial solutions for investors etc. If you are really good you can even earn a contract (according to their site, this can mean more than $100.000 a year). But let's stay realistic. When your article gets accepted they'll pay you 50$. If it's really top-notch, you will be paid 100$ per post.

118. www.postloop.com . Their slogan is "we make money-making fun". Earn money by posting at forums and blogs. Forum and blog owners sometimes need to attract visitors to bootstrap their traffic. This site acts as an intermediate between blog and forum owners and people that want to comment on these blogs and forums. You comment on a blog and you get paid through PayPal.

119. www.demandstudios.com . This is the company behind the huge how-to site, eHow. They are always searching for unique content on business, technology, careers, family, parenting, travel, fitness, nutrition, science, home, gardening, real estate, pets , cars etc. Over 100 million visitors per month on their different sites (AZcentarl.com, Globalpost, legalzoom etc.)

120. PayPerPost. http://www.payperpost.com/ . As the name suggests, here you can go to monetize your blog, twitter, instagram or FB account. Advertisers create "opportunities" on PayPerPost (PPP). The blogger then chooses the opportunity ("opps"). Once the blogger has written a blog post or made a video, PPP reviews it against its requirements and handles payment.

121. Smorty. www.smorty.com This site works in a very similar way as PayPerPost. It functions as a community between bloggers and advertisers. For a full listing of their rules , check out this page http://www.smorty.com/g/7165/blogger-rules.html

122. Another way of using your writing skills to make money, is writing PLR material. (Private Label Rights). You write PLR articles or eBooks which you can sell on PLR sites. People who are short of ideas or time or both might be interested to buy your articles/eBooks from you.

Write eBooks

Writing eBooks, like the one you are reading, can also be a very lucrative business. You can write an eBook on a topic that interests you, and for which there is a demand, and sell it on Kindle on Amazon.

As with the other topics, let's stay realistic. The probability that you will write another Stephen King book or a Harry Potter with your first book is close to zero. The only way that you can make money by writing books, is by writing many of them.

Take an niche that interests you and think about the topics that you could write about. If you can get up with at least 10 ideas it might be interesting to dig further.

The math is pretty simple. Let's say you write en eBook that sells a couple of books a day for $1-3$ on which you make, let's say $1. So a conservative guestimate is 5-10 $ a day. That's already not bad, because if you multiply this with 30 days, that could mean $200-$300. No, that's not enough to create a fulltime income.

But let's say you write 10 books. You will create synergy between these books and, if your books are interesting , you may create over time a loyal audience. And now you are talking about a couple of thousand dollars a month !

Again, there is no shortcut here. You can make a comfortable income by writing eBooks, but it will take a lot of time and effort.

Books can be classified in two main categories. Fiction and non-fiction. Fiction is, in my opinion, much more difficult to write, because you have to have a lot of imagination. You have to invent the whole story, the characters, the locations, the dialogues etc. etc.

Non-fiction books have a completely other approach. Here, the key to success is : research. Most people will tell you that if you write non-fiction books, you should take a topic that interests you and that you are knowledgeable about.

I don't agree with that. I could write a book about 'how to create the perfect lawn', even if I have no knowledge about gardening whatsoever. By doing extensive research in books, forums, blogs, I could probably hammer out a book like that in a month.

Sure, you cannot just take any topic. It would be impossible to write a book 'how to become a heart surgeon', because the subject is far too large and far too complicated to master in a short time.

But you can start of by thinking about your hobbies, your interests and write one or more books about it. Here are some pointers in the right direction to get you going in the eBook business.

123. Subscribe to the Amazon Kindle Publishing on kdp.amazon.com . Create your book and upload it to Amazon. You set the price yourself. Kindle publishing is a huge subject on itself. Start out by reading all the information on the page mentioned above. Your royalties on a book sale will be 35% or 70% depending on the price you set for your book.

Section 5 : Sell advertising

When you have a website you can sell advertising space. Advertisers will pay you, depending on the niche or topic of your site, the number of visitors etc. The more visitors you get to your site, the more ads will be clicked, and the more you will be paid.

124. One of the most well-known ways to make some money with your website is Adsense. https://www.google.com/adsense . This is the advertising network for publishers ran by Google. Signup with a Google account, create space on your site to display Google ads. Choose what type of ads can compete for that space. Advertisers compete for your space with a bid like in a real-time auction. Google will then display the highest paying ad. You will get 68% of the revenue. You can also make money with Adsense by putting up a Google searchbar on your site. Every time that a visitor uses the Google search bar on your site, and clicks on one of the ads in the search results, you will get paid.

125. Signup with https://www.jebbit.com as a publisher. Put an ad on your site. Jebbit will put an "explore" button on your site. When a visitor clicks the explore button, a destination webpage is overlaid with a question that entices the consumer to explore the content further. The consumer interacts with the webpage content, answering questions as they are driven to a specific action or goal. Finally, consumers are rewarded with a branded coupon, cash or other prize for correctly completing a series of questions and actions.

126. Sell Banner space on your site. You will need a significant number of visitors to your site to make this work. The price you can charge depends on the location where you will put your banners.

A banner on the top of your home page is worth much more then near the bottom or on an internal page. To get banners from potential advertisers you will have to search for advertisers that have products in your niche. One of the best one is :

127. BuySellads. www.buysellads.com . This is one of the bigger sites where advertisers and publishers meet.

Section 6 : Phone apps

Do you have a mobile phone? I know, pretty stupid question in our civilized world. Now instead of just paying for your phone and your subscription, start using it to make some cash !

128. Download the iPhone or Android app from www.gigwalk.com . Open the app and click on the red dots around the location where you are. Every dot is a small task which makes you some money. This can be taking pictures of buildings, inside shops, mystery shopping, testing mobile apps and more.

129. www.fieldagent.net works in a similar way as gigwalk. Download the app for iPhone and pick up a task. This can be a price survey in a local Wal-Mart, filling out a survey or double-checking information on a website.

130. www.shopkick.com is a mobile app that pays for shopping, regardless if you buy something or not. It shows you popular products and rewards waiting for you at stores like Target, Macy's, Best Buy, Old Navy, American Eagle, JCPenney, Sports Authority and Crate & Barrel. And it rewards you with kicks (points) just for walking in the door. Get even more kicks when you scan items and make purchases. Redeem your points for gift cards at your favorite stores. Now you can do even more of what you love—shop

131. www.checkpoints.com . The company compensates you with points and rewards for checking in at different stores, scanning items, playing games, watch videos or completing offers. Points can be exchanged for discounts, gift cards from Amazon, Target, WalMart and much more.

132. www.easyshiftapp.com . This site is very similar to gigwalk. Get paid cash to shop, eat and explore in your city. Here the tasks are called "shifts". You can do the shifts at your convenience. This can be : taking a picture, recording a price, etc. Only available for iPhone

133. www.apptrailers.com : Android and iPhone. Preview video trailers and get points that you can redeem with PayPal cash, Amazon gift codes. The videos are trailers for new apps. So you get informed about new apps that will be launched soon.

Section 7 : Content revenue sharing

Revenue sharing is the concept, where you publish content on a site (article, video, eBook etc.), the site displays ads with your content. The site gets paid by its advertisers and this revenue gets shared with you. Sometimes 50-50 and others may give you up to 70% or more.

The good thing about this concept is that you don't need to create a website yourself, maintain it, promoting it, getting traffic etc. Most of these sites are huge and popular, so you will get decent traffic to your content (if it is good), as soon as you publish it.

The downside is that you are building your business on someone else's site. So if one day they decide to close shop, all your work will be gone. If you're in it for the long haul, I would suggest that you create your own website so that you have complete control over the contents.

If you don't feel ready to start your own website, then working with revenue sharing sites is a great option. And of course, nothing prevents you from doing both.

134. YouTube. www.youtube.com . By far, the most popular and most visited video website on the internet. Owned by Google. The principle is pretty simple. You post a video. If you get enough visitors to your video, or subscribers to your channel, you strike an advertisement deal with YouTube.

Notice that you will have to collect millions of views to get to this level. But there are examples of numerous young people who create regularly new videos in which they review products, or imitate the latest hit in a funny way. When you can create something funny, and you can repeat it, you can become a YouTube star!

135. You can also use YouTube to make videos that have the only objective to get viewers to an affiliate offer or to your own site.
Squidoo : www.squidoo.com. Pages on squidoo are called 'lenses'. You create a page (or lens) on squidoo and include your affiliate links or Google Adsense ads to monetize your pages.

136. Hubpages. www.hubpages.com . If you like writing you can post your efforts on hubpages. Probably one of the most popular revenue-sharing article websites.

137. infobarrel. www.infobarrel.com . Here you can also post your articles and share the revenues. Some authors earn a very respectable income on this site after having published hundreds of articles.

138. webanswers. www.webanswers.com . Answer questions on all kinds of topics. Gardening, Business, Arts, cars, pets, legal etc. Create an account. Once you have answered 50 questions, you will be invited to open a Google Adsense account.

Your goal is to have users select your answer as "the best answer". If your answer is selected as "the best answer" you will earn ongoing advertising royalties on that thread and this question becomes yours to monetize. The more "best answers" you receive the more money you earn.

139. Bestreviewer : www.best-reviewers.com . If you are good in writing TOP X lists, then this site is for you. Write a top X list on any topic and post it here. For example 'Top 10 Cell Phones'. 'Top 5 stocks to buy'. Get a Google Adsense account. For each 'TOP' you create, a page will be created with up to 3 Adsense blocks with your Adsense publisher ID.

Section 8 : Miscellaneous

In this section I have included a mixed bag of things that I couldn't fit in any of the other sections.

Get paid to watch TV

140. RewardTV. Watch your daily shows as you normally would do. Then go to www.rewardtv.com and signup. Answer trivia questions about the shows . You can earn points and prizes like free gas, game consoles

141. Viggle. https://viggleinc.com/ . Check-in and choose between TV or music. If you check-in for TV you earn 1 point for every minute you're checked in. Get extra bonus points for sharing shows. Earn additional points for getting your friends sign up to Viggle. Redeem your points for electronics, trips, and gift cards. One of the best apps of 2012 according to Techcrunch.

Paid focus groups

Businesses are always looking for ways to improve their products, and find new products to blow the competition away. There are lots of opportunities to participate in these focus groups.

Focus groups are often organized locally in a physical location. Thus you have to live in the specific area to participate. But there are some sites that conduct online focus groups.

142. 2020panel : www.2020panel.com . Get paid to share your opinion. By giving your honest opinion and insight, you help companies to improve and develop better products for the marketplace. You could be paid $50, $150 or more just for sharing your opinion.

143. FindFocusGroups. www.findfocusgroups.com . Another site where you can find focusgroups by city or state. Sign up, find a paid focus group in your area, participate, and get paid !

Buy and sell websites

Buying and selling websites can be a very lucrative business. However, it is not something that I would recommend to beginners. There are lots of criteria that you should take into account when buying or selling a website.

Actually, the subject is so vast, that it would require a complete book to explain all the issues involved in buying and selling websites. For completeness, I have included some sites that are dealing with trading websites.

144. Flippa. www.flippa.com . Flippa is a site where people can buy and sell websites. If you want to make a quick start, you can have a look here to see if there isn't a site that is already created and that has potential. There are sites that you can pickup for $1 !! Check out how they rate in Google, the number of backlinks they have, what their competitors are, their age. Run them through ahrefs and opensiteexplorer.

If you can build up the audience, you can resell your site later on for a nice profit. Buying and selling websites is not something that you would start with. It is a very fast subject. But remember that a website, as far as its value is concerned, is exactly the same as a brick and mortar shop.

If your site has a huge number of visitors and creates lots of revenue, you can sell it, just like you would sell a shop in the real world. Some sites have been sold for millions of dollars !

145. Trustiu. https://www.trustiu.com/ . This site also allows you to buy and sell websites, domain names. You can also park domains here. Hundreds of websites for sale .

146. Website   broker. http://www.websitebroker.com/. This is a much smaller site where you can buy and sell websites. Less than a hundred for sale.
    .

147. https://www.justwebsitebrokerage.com/ Buy and sell websites

148. https://digitalexits.com/website-broker-incomediary/ Digital Exits is our #1 recommended website broker. They represent websites making $100k – $5m a year in profit. They are best if you have an established business over 2 years old making at least $100,000 per year

149. https://empireflippers.com/ is by far the largest vetted private marketplace. They do preliminary vetting of each deal to ensure the traffic, P&L, seller intent, among other things is correct. You still need to vet the deal to match your criteria.

150. Create podcasts. A podcast is an audio recording. Some bloggers use podcasts in their blogs. Or they do audio transcription from a written text (or the other way around). Some people like to read, others like to listen. If you can offer both you will attract more people, which means more sales and more money.

Take Action

Well, here you have it. 150 ways to make money online. From very simple 'download an app on your phone and take a picture' to 'create a full blown membership site'.

When I started out I had around 250 ideas. But I think that 150 ideas for a couple of cents per idea is already big value for money. If you want to have more, drop me a mail, and I'll consider a second volume . ☺

As I pointed out, even in a life time you won't have time to try them all out. Take a couple of ideas that suit best with your objectives, in time effort and how far you want to take this.

But the most important thing is : **TAKE ACTION** . You can put this book aside, and start reading another one, and another one, but the best way to learn what works (and what not) is by doing it !

Sure, you will make mistakes, and not everything you try will work out. But it is enough to get one or two things working really very good to make a decent income on the internet.

Thank you

Thank you for having read my book till the end. I hope you liked it and that you have learned what you were looking for.

If you have appreciated my book I would like to ask you just ONE favor. Please leave me an honest review on Amazon . You can click here

If you got this book for free during a promotion period, I would highly appreciate it if you could leave me an honest review.

It will only take you a minute or two. I value any feedback from you. If it is really positive, I have attained my objective of adding real value in my book for you. If it is average or less, I can use your feedback to make it better. I wish you lots of success in your online activities.

Timo

About the Author

Biography

Timo is a writer, blogger and IT expert. He writes about complex things, like keyword research, affiliate marketing and online marketing. But in a language that is understandable for everybody.

He uses 30+ years experience in computers, networking, hardware, software, development, internet, marketing, sales and online business to teach others how to grasp complex issues. His international experience, working abroad in several European countries, US and Africa has given him a broad view on different cultures and civilizations.

He has followed the development of the internet right from the start. In the 80's just with email and private networks, and from the early 90's onwards he was one of the first ones to work with the first websites.

Learn from the author how to setup an online business, how to understand everything about search engines, how to create your own 'internet life-style'.

His books are extremely results-oriented: You are looking for a solution to a specific problem? When you read a book from the author, you will find the answer.

In straight-to-the-point explanations without the fluff.

When Timo is not writing or blogging he spends his time on the magnificent beaches between St Tropez and Monaco, relaxing in a pub in Cannes, playing chess or travelling to his home country : The Netherlands.

All Books from the Author

Here are all my books:

- 150 Ways to Make Money Online. Learn How to Make Hard Cash with Your Computer from Home

- Find Golden Keywords with FREE software. Dig up Golden Nuggets with Google Keyword Planner.

- The Ultimate Kindle Formatting Guide. From Word to Kindle. Better Formatting = More Sales

- How to Make Money with eBooks. The Best Collection of Marketing Tactics to Boost Your Sales.

- Amazon Reviews Exposed. The Truth about Amazon Reviews.

- The Complete Book Cover Creation Guide. What makes a good cover and how to create your own for FREE.

- How to Make Book Covers that Sell. Everything You Need to Know About Book Cover Design. (Part I of The Complete Book Cover Creation Guide).

- How to Create Professional Book Covers. Make Your Own Free Book Covers Free With GIMP. (Part II of The Complete Book Cover Creation Guide)

- How To Find Niche Markets That Sell. A complete guide to niche marketing resources. This is a FREE download.

Disclaimer

This product is not legal or accounting advice. The author has made all efforts to be as accurate as possible. Due to the continuously changing nature of the internet, some references mentioned in this book may change and may not work anymore. The author shall not be liable for any loss incurred as a consequence of the use and application of any information presented in this book.

The author has no control over the content, nature and availability of the websites mentioned in this book. References to these sites do not imply a recommendation or endorsement by the author.

While every attempt has been made to check and verify the information in this book, the author does not assume any responsibility for errors, omissions or contrary interpretation of the subject matter herein.

Earning claims mentioned anywhere in this product are completely dependent on the time and effort invested, and are in no way guaranteed.

The author and the affiliates of this book are not liable for any damages or losses associated with the content of this book.